U0111776

大展好書　好書大展
品嘗好書　冠群可期

大展好書　好書大展
品嘗好書　冠群可期

▲作者的少林拳　Shaolin Boxing of the Author

▲武術雜誌上的耿軍
Geng Jun on the Cover of Wushu Magazine

▲英法武術代表團訪問孟州少林武術院
The Wushu Delegation of France and UK is visiting the Meng zhou Shaolin Wushu Institute

▲作者部分弟子參加武打片拍攝
Parts of students of author take part in fliming Acrobatic fighting film

▲作者與恩師素法大師
The Author and his Teacher Grandmaster Sufa

▲作者指導女兒耿瑞濤練功
The Author is coaching his daughter to practise her skill

▲作者與原國家武術協會主席張耀庭
The Author and the former Chairman of the Chinese Wushu Association Zhang Yaoting

▲作者的少林拳　Shaolin Boxing of the Author

▲ 武術雜誌封面上的耿軍
Geng Jun on the Cover of Wushu Magazine

▲ 作者與恩師素法大師
The Author and his Teacher Grandmaster Sufa

▲作者率領國外弟子朝拜少林寺　Author leads foreign students to visit Shaolin Temple

▲作者與武僧教頭德揚師兄在捶譜堂
In Chuipu Hall, the author and his senior fellow apprentice
who is also the wushu monk teacher deyang

▲作者與中國政協副主席萬國權
The Author and the vice Chairman of the Chinese People's Political
Consultative Conference（CPPCC）Wan Guoquan

▲ 作者傳藝國際黑帶功夫總會
The Author is teaching his Wushu skill in International
Black Belt Kungfu Federation

▲ 作者指導兒子耿鵬飛練功
The Author is coaching his son Geng Pengfei to practise
his skill

少林傳統功夫漢英對照系列　❸

Shaolin Traditional Kungfu Series Books　❸

七星螳螂拳

Shaolin Seven-star Mantis Boxing（White-Ape Offering Fruit）

白猿獻果

耿　軍　著

Written by Geng Jun

大展出版社有限公司

作者簡介

　　耿軍（法號釋德君），1968 年 11 月出生於河南省孟州市，係少林寺三十一世皈依弟子。中國武術七段、全國十佳武術教練員、中國少林武術研究會副秘書長、焦作市政協十屆常委、濟南軍區特警部隊特邀武功總教練、洛陽師範學院客座教授、英才教育集團董事長。1989 年創辦孟州少林武術院、2001 年創辦英才雙語學校。先後獲得河南省優秀青年新聞人物、全國優秀武術教育家等榮譽稱號。

　　1983 年拜在少林寺住持素喜法師和著名武僧素法大師門下學藝，成爲大師的關門弟子，後經素法大師引薦，又隨螳螂拳一代宗師李占元、金剛力功于憲華等大師學藝。在中國鄭州國際少林武術節、全國武林精英大賽、全國武術演武大會等比賽中 6 次獲得少林武術冠軍；在中華傳統武術精粹大賽中獲得了象徵少林武術最高榮譽的「達摩杯」一座。他主講示範的 36 集《少林傳統功夫》教學片已由人民體育音像出版社出版發行。他曾多次率團出訪海外，在國際武術界享有較高聲譽。

　　他創辦的孟州少林武術院，現已發展成爲豫北地區最大的以學習文化爲主、以武術爲辦學特色的封閉式、寄宿制學校，是中國十大武術教育基地之一。

Brief Introduction to the Author

Geng Jun (also named Shidejun in Buddhism) , born in Mengzhou City of Henan Province, November 1968, is a Bud –dhist disciple of the 31st generation, the 7th section of Chinese Wu shu, national "Shijia" Wu shu coach, Vice Secretary General of China Shaolin Wu shu Research Society, standing committee member of 10th Political Consultative Conference of Jiaozuo City, invited General Kungfu Coach of special police of Jinan Military District, visiting professor of Luoyang Normal University, and Board Chairman of Yingcai Education Group. In 1989, he estab –lished Mengzhou Shaolin Wu shu Institute; in 2001, he estab –lished Yingcai Bilingual School · He has been successively awarded honorable titles of "Excellent Youth News Celebrity of Henan Province" "State Excellent Wu shu Educationalist" etc.

In 1983, he learned Wu shu from Suxi Rabbi, the Abbot of Shaolin Temple, and Grandmaster Sufa, a famous Wu shu monk, and became the last disciple of the

Grandmaster. Then recom–mended by Grandmaster Sufa, he learned Wu shu from masters such as Li Zhanyuan, great master of mantis boxing, and Yu Xianhua who specializes in Jingangli gong. He won the Shaolin Wu shu champion for 6 times in China Zhengzhou International Wu shu Festival, National Competition of Wu lin Elites, National Wu shu Performance Conference, etc. and one "Damo Trophy" that symbolizes the highest honor of Shaolin Wu shu in Chinese Traditional Wu shu Succinct Competition. 36 volumes teaching VCD of Shaolin Traditional Wu shu has been published and is –sued by People´s Sports Audio Visual Publishing House. He has led delegations to visit overseas for many times, enjoying high reputation in the martial art circle of the world.

Mengzhou Shaolin Wu shu Institute, established by him, has developed into the largest enclosed type boarding school of Yubei (north of Henan Province) area, which takes knowledge as primary and Wu shu as distinctiveness, also one of China´s top ten Wu shu education bases.

序　言

　　中華武術源遠流長，門類繁多。

　　少林武術源自嵩山少林寺，因寺齊名，是我國拳系中著名的流派之一。少林寺自北魏太和十九年建寺以來，已有一千五百多年的歷史。而少林武術也決不是哪一人哪一僧所獨創，它是歷代僧俗歷經漫長的生活歷程，根據生活所需逐步豐富完善而成。

　　據少林寺志記載許多少林僧人在出家之前就精通武術或慕少林之名而來或迫於生計或看破紅塵等諸多原因削髮爲僧投奔少林，少林寺歷來倡武，並經常派武僧下山，雲遊四方尋師學藝。還請武林高手到寺，如宋朝的福居禪師曾邀集十八家武林名家到寺切磋技藝，推動了少林武術的發展，使少林武術得諸家之長。

　　本書作者自幼習武，師承素喜、素法和螳螂拳李占元等多位名家，當年如饑似渴在少林寺研習功夫，曾多次在國內外大賽中獲獎。創辦的孟州少林武術院亦是全國著名的武術院校之一，他示範主講的 36 集《少林傳統功夫》教學 VCD 已由人民體育音像出版社發行。

　　本套叢書的三十多個少林傳統套路和實戰技法是少

七星螳螂拳白猿獻果

林武術的主要内容，部分還是作者獨到心得，很值得一讀，該書還採用漢英文對照，使外國愛好者無語言障礙，爲少林武術走向世界做出了自己的貢獻，亦是可喜可賀之事。

張耀庭題
甲申秋月

Preface

Chinese Wushu is originated from ancient time and has a long history, it has various styles.

Shaolin Wushu named from the Shaolin Temple of Songshan Mountain, it is one of the famous styles in the Chinese boxing genre. Shaolin temple has more than 1500 years of history since its establishment in the 19th year of North Wei Taihe Dynasty. No one genre of Shaolin Wushu is created solely by any person or monk, but completed gradually by Buddhist monks and common people from generation to generation through long-lasting living course according to the requirements of life. As recording of Record of Shaolin Temple, many Shaolin Buddhist monks had already got a mastery of Wushu before they became a Buddhist monk, they came to Shaolin for tonsure to be a Buddhist monk due to many reasons such as admiring for the name of Shaolin, or by force of life or seeing through thevanity of life. The Shaolin Temple always promotes Wushu and frequently appoints Wushu Buddhist monks to go down the mountain to roam around for searching masters and learning Wushu from them. It also invites

Wushu experts to come to the temple, such as Buddhist monk Fuju of Song Dynasty, it once invited Wushu famous exports of 18 schools to come to the temple to make skill interchange, which promoted the development of Shaolin Wushu and made it absorb advantages of all other schools.

The author learned from many famous exports such as Suxi, Sufa and Li Zhanyuan of Mantis Boxing, he studied Chinese boxing eagerly in Shaolin Temple, and got lots of awards both at home and abroad, he also set up the Mengzhou Shaolin Wushu Institute, which is one of the most famous Wushu institutes around China. He makes demonstration and teaching in the 36 volumes teaching VCD of Shaolin Traditional Wushu, which have been published by Peoples sports Audio Visual publishing house.

There are more than 30 traditional Shaolin routines and practical techniques in this series of books, which are the main content of Shaolin Wushu, and part of which is the original things learned by the author, it is worthy of reading. The series books adopt Chinese and English versions, make foreign fans have no language barrier, and make contribution to Shaolin Wushu going to the world, which is delighting and congratulating thing.

Titled by Zhang Yaoting

目　錄
Contents

說　明

（一）為了表述清楚，以圖像和文字對動作作了分解說明，練習時應力求連貫銜接。

（二）在文字說明中，除特別說明外，不論先寫或後寫身體的某一部分，各運動部位都要求協調活動、連貫銜接，切勿先後割裂。

（三）動作方向轉變以人體為準，標明前後左右。

（四）圖上的線條是表明這一動作到下一動作經過的線路及部位。左手、左腳及左轉均為虛線（┈┈►）；右手、右腳及右轉均為實線（──►）。

七星螳螂拳白猿獻果

Instructions

(i) In order to explain clearly figures and words are used to describe the actions in multi steps. Try to keep coherent when exercising.

(ii) In the word instruction, unless special instruction, each action part of the body shall act harmoniously and join coherently no matter it is written first or last, please do not separate the actions.

(iii) The action direction shall be turned taking body as standard, which is marked with front, back, left or right.

(iv) The line in the figure shows the route and position from this action to the next action. The left hand, left foot and turn left are all showed in broken line (------►) ; the right hand, right foot and turn right are all showed in real line (——►) .

基本步型與基本手型
Basic stances and Basic hand forms

圖 1

圖 2

圖 3

圖 4

圖 5

圖 6

七星螳螂拳白猿獻果

圖 7

圖 8

圖 9

圖 10

圖 11

圖 12

圖 13

圖 14

圖 15

圖 16

圖 17

圖 18

圖 19

圖 20

圖 21

基本步型與基本手型

基本步型

少林武術中常見的步型有：弓步、馬步、仆步、虛步、歇步、坐盤步、丁步、併步、七星步、跪步、高虛步、翹腳步 12 種。

弓步：俗稱弓箭步。兩腿前後站立，兩腳相距本人腳長的 4～5 倍；前腿屈至大腿接近水平，腳尖微內扣不超過 5°；後腿伸膝挺直，腳掌內扣 45°。（圖 1）

馬步：俗稱騎馬步。兩腳開立，相距本人腳長的 3～3.5 倍，兩腳尖朝前；屈膝下蹲大腿接近水平，膝蓋與兩腳尖上下成一條線。（圖 2）

仆步：俗稱單叉，一腿屈膝全蹲，大腿貼緊小腿，膝微外展，另一腿直伸平仆接近地面，腳掌扣緊與小腿成 90°夾角。（圖 3）

虛步：又稱寒雞步。兩腳前後站立，前後相距本人腳長的 2 倍；重心移至後腿，後腿屈膝下蹲至大腿接近水平，腳掌外擺 45°；前腿腳尖點地，兩膝相距 10 公分。（圖 4）

歇步：兩腿左右交叉，靠近全蹲；前腳全腳掌著地，腳尖外展，後腳腳前掌著地，臀部微坐於後腿小腿上。（圖 5）

坐盤步：在歇步的形狀下，坐於地上，後腿的大小腿外側和腳背均著地。（圖 6）

丁步：兩腿併立，屈膝下蹲，大腿接近水平，一腳尖點地靠近另一腳內側腳窩處。（圖 7）

併步：兩腿併立，屈膝下蹲，大腿接近水平。（圖 8）

七星步：七星步是少林七星拳和大洪拳中獨有的步型。一腳內側腳窩內扣於另一腳腳尖，兩腿屈膝下蹲，接近水平。（圖 9）

跪步：又稱小蹬山步。兩腳前後站立，相距本人腳長的 2.5 倍，前腿屈膝下蹲，後腿下跪，接近地面，後腳腳跟離地。（圖 10）

高虛步：又稱高點步。兩腳前後站立，重心後移，後腿腳尖外擺 45°，前腿腳尖點地，兩腳尖相距一腳距離。（圖 11）

翹腳步：在七星螳螂拳中又稱七星步，兩腿前後站立，相距本人腳長的 1.5 倍，後腳尖外擺 45°，屈膝下蹲，前腿直伸，腳跟著地，腳尖微內扣。（圖 12）

基本手型

少林武術中常見的手型有拳、掌、鉤 3 種。

拳：

分為平拳和透心拳。

平拳：平拳是武術中較普遍的一種拳型，又稱方拳。四指屈向手心握緊，拇指橫屈扣緊食指。（圖

13）

透心拳：此拳主要用於打擊心窩處，故名。四指併攏捲握，中指突出拳面，拇指扣緊抵壓中指梢節處。（圖14）

掌：

分為柳葉掌、八字掌、虎爪掌、鷹爪掌、鉗指掌。

柳葉掌：四指併立，拇指內扣。（圖15）

八字掌：四指併立，拇指張開。（圖16）

虎爪掌：五指分開，彎曲如鉤，形同虎爪。（圖17）

鷹爪掌：又稱鎖喉手，拇指內扣，小指和無名指彎曲扣於掌心處，食指和中指分開內扣。（圖18）

鉗指掌：五指分開，掌心內含。（圖19）

鉤：

分為鉤手和螳螂鉤。

鉤手：屈腕，五指自然內合，指尖相攏。此鉤使用較廣，武術中提到的鉤均為此鉤。（圖20）

螳螂鉤：又稱螳螂爪，屈腕成腕部上凸，無名指、小指屈指內握，食指、中指內扣，拇指梢端按貼於食指中節。（圖21）

Basic stances

基本步型與基本手型

Usual stances in Shaolin Wushu are: bow stance, horse stance, crouch stance, empty stance, rest stance, cross – legged sitting, T – stance, feet – together stance, seven – star stance, kneel stance, high empty stance, and toes – raising stance, these twelve kinds.

Bow stance: commonly named bow – and – arrow stance. Two feet stand in tandem, the distance between two feet is about four or five times of length of one´s foot; the front leg bends to the extent of the thigh nearly horizontal with toes slightly turned inward by less than 5°; the back leg stretches straight with the sole turned inward by 45°. (Figure 1)

Horse stance: commonly named riding step. two feet stand apart, the distance between two feet is 3~3.5 times of length of one´s foot, with tiptoes turned forward; bend knees to squat downward, with thighs nearly horizontal, knees and two tiptoes in line. (Figure 2)

Crouch stance: commonly named single split. Bend the knee of one leg and squat entirely with thigh very close to lower leg and knee outspread slightly; straighten the other leg and crouch horizontally close to floor, keep the sole turned inward and forming an included angle of 90° with lower leg. (Figure 3)

Empty stance: also named cold – chicken stance. Two feet stand in tandem, the distance between two feet is 2 times of

length of one´s foot; transfer the barycenter to back leg, bend the knee of the back leg and squat downward to the extent of the thigh nearly horizontal, with the sole turned outward by 45°; keep the tiptoe of front leg on the ground, with distance between two knees of 10cm. (Figure 4)

Rest stance: cross the two legs at left and right, keep them close and entirely squat; keep the whole sole of the front foot on the ground with tiptoes turned outward, the front sole of the back foot on the ground, and buttocks slightly seated on the lower leg of the back leg. (Figure 5)

Cross–legged sitting: in the posture of rest stance, sit on the ground, with the outer sides of the thigh and lower leg of the back leg and instep on the ground. (Figure 6)

T–stance: two legs stand with feet together, bend knees and squat to the extent of the thighs nearly horizontal, with one tiptoe on the ground and close to inner side of the fossa of the other foot. (Figure 7)

Feet–together stance: two legs stand with feet together, bend knees and squat to the extent of the thigh nearly horizontal. (Figure 8)

Seven–star stance: Seven–star step is a unique step form in Shaolin Seven–star Boxing and Major Flood Boxing. Keep the inner side of the fossa of one foot turned inward onto tiptoe of the other foot, bend two knees and squat nearly horizontal. (Figure 9)

Kneel stance: also named small mountaineering stance. Two feet stand in tandem, the distance between two feet is 2.5

times of length of one´s foot, bend knee of the front leg and squat, kneel the back leg close to the floor, with the heel of back foot off the floor. (Figure 10)

High empty stance: also named high point stance. Two feet stand in tandem. Transfer the barycenter backward, turn the tiptoe of the back leg outward by 45°, with tiptoe of front leg on the ground, and the distance between two tiptoes is length of one foot. (Figure 11)

Toes −raising stance: also named seven −star stance in Seven−star Mantis Boxing. Two legs stand in tandem, and the distance between two legs is 1.5 times of length of one´s foot. Keep the tiptoe of back leg turned outward by 45°, bend knees and squat, straighten the front leg with heel on the ground and tiptoe turned inward slightly. (Figure 12)

Basic hand forms

Usual hand forms in Shaolin Wushu are: fist, palm and hook, these three kinds.

Fist: classified into straight fist and heart−penetrating fist.

Flat fist: a rather common fist form in Wushu, also named square fist. Hold the four fingers tightly toward the palm, and horizontally bend the thumb to button up the fore finger. (Figure 13)

Heart−penetrating fist: mainly used for striking the heart part. Put four fingers together and coil−hold them, the middle finger thrusts out the striking surface of the fist, the thumb

buttons up and presses the end and joint of the middle finger. (Figure 14)

Palm: classified into willow leaf palm, splay palm, tiger's claw palm, eagle's claw palm, fingers clamping palm.

Willow leaf palm: palm with four fingers up and thumb turned inward. (Figure 15)

Eight – shape palm: palm with four fingers up and thumb splay. (Figure 16)

Tiger's claw palm: palm with five fingers apart, bent as hook and like tiger's claw. (Figure 17)

Eagle's claw palm: also named throat locking hand, with the thumb turned inward, the little finger and middle finger turned onto palm, fore finger and middle finger apart and turned inward. (Figure 18)

Fingers clamp palm: palm with five fingers apart and palm drawn in. (Figure 19)

Hook: classified into hook hand and mantis hook.

Hook hand: bend the wrist, five fingers drawn in naturally with fingertips together. This hook is used in wide range, the hook mentioned in Wushu refers to this. (Figure 20)

Mantis hook: also named mantis' claw, bend wrist into wrist bulge upward, the ring finger and little finger bend to hold inward, with fore finger and fore middle finger turned inward and end of thumb pressed on the middle joint of the fore finger. (Figure 21)

白猿獻果套路簡介

Brief Introduction to the Routine White Ape Offering Fruit

七星螳螂拳是清初拳師王郎在研究螳螂捕蟬時運用兩臂劈、砍、刁、閃的捕鬥技巧而創編的一種象形拳法。後王郎入少林寺 3 年，向寺僧傳授螳螂拳法。白猿獻書是七星螳螂拳其中的一個套路，該套路剛柔並濟、長短互用、手到腳到、貫穿緊湊、節奏明快、勁整力圓、周身相合、勾摟纏封、變化無窮。

Seven–star mantis boxing is a kind of shape – simulating boxing, which was developed and compiled by Wang Lang, a boxer at early Qing Dynasty, applying the capturing and fighting skills of the two arms when he researched the scene of mantis capturing cicada. Later, Wang Lang stayed at Shao Temple for 3 years, and taught mantis boxing to the monks of this temple. White Ape Offering Fruit is one of the routines in seven–star mantis boxing, which uses the temper force with grace, both long and short actions, harmonious and consistent actions of the hands and feet, forthright rhythm, integral strength and complete force, the actions of hook, grad, twining and closing, being coherent, compact and most changeful.

白猿獻果套路動作名稱

Action Names of Routine White Ape Offering Fruit

第一段　Section One

1. 按掌預備勢

   Preparatory posture with pressing palm

2. 仙人指路

   Immortals points to way

3. 霸王甩鞭

   Overlord swings whip

4. 圈捶

   Circle hammer

5. 格肘上步戳捶

   Parry with elbow, step forward and thrust hammer

6. 左封右崩捶

   Left wrap and right snap hammer

7. 撩陰捶

   Upper-cut croth with hammer

8. 轉身圈捶秘肘

   Turn about and circular hammer with secret elbow

第二段　Section Two

9. 轉身掄劈提剁

   Turn over, swing, hack, lift and chop

10. 三抹眉

   Smear eyebrow three times

11. 蓋陽掌玉環步

   Cover with Yang-palm in jade-ring step

12. 左封右崩捶

   Left wrap and right snap hammer

13. 千眼鴛鴦腳

   Thousand-eye mandarin duck foot

14. 閉手

   Close-up hand

15. 左右紉針

   Thread needle to the left and right

16. 玉環步

   Jade-ring step

第三段　Section Three

17. 轉身霸王甩鞭

   Overlord turns and swings whip

18. 左封右崩捶

   Left wrap and right snap hammer

19. 採三手玉環步

Grab hand three times in jade－ring step

第四段　Section Four

20. 轉身連環戳捶

Turn around and thrust interlink hammer

21. 左封右崩捶

Left wrap and right snap hammer

22. 採三手玉環步

Grab hand three times in jade－ring step

23. 橫掃千軍雙封手

Sweep and wrap with hands

24. 收　勢

Closing form

白猿獻果套路動作圖解
Action Illustrations of Routine White Ape Offering Fruit

圖1

第一段　Section One

1. 按掌預備勢
Preparatory posture with pressing palm

(1)兩腳併立；兩手自然下垂，五指併攏，貼於體側；目視前方。（圖1）

(1)Stand with feet together, two hands drop naturally with five fingers putting together and close to the sides of the body. Eyes look forward.（Figure 1）

圖2

（2）兩掌翻掌，掌心向上，從身體兩側緩緩向上托掌，托至頭上方時兩臂屈肘，向胸前緩緩按掌，兩掌心向下，掌指相對，高與肩平；目視前方。（圖2、圖2附圖）

白猿獻果套路動作圖解

圖 2 附圖

(2) Turn over two palms into the palms up, lift the palms upward slowly from two sides of the body. Bend elbows of two arms when lifting overhead, then press the palms to the front of the chest slowly. With two palms down, the fingers opposite at the shoulder level. Eyes look forward. (Figure 2, Attached figure 2)

圖 3

(3)上動不停。下身姿勢不變；雙掌繼續向下按掌，落於小腹前，兩掌心均向下，掌指相對；目視前方。（圖 3、圖 3 附圖）

　　要點：挺胸塌腰，頭正頸直，雙掌上托、下按要與呼吸配合。

圖 3 附圖

(3) Keep the above action, make the lower part of the body unchangeable, continue to press the two palms downward and fall to the front of the lower abdomen with two palms down and the fingers opposite. Eyes look forward. ﹝ Figure 3, Attached figure 3 ﹞

Key points: keep chest out and waist downward, head being correctitude and neck straight, lift the two palms upward and cooperate with the breath on pressing the palms.

圖 4

2. 仙人指路　Immortals points to way

(1)接上勢。右腳向前上一步，腳尖外擺，左腿屈膝，腳跟離地；同時，左掌變拳收抱於腰間，拳心向上；右掌前伸，向外翻腕採抓變螳螂鉤，鉤尖向下，高與肩平；目視前方。（圖4）

白
猿
獻
果
套
路
動
作
圖
解

(1) Follow the above posture, the right foot takes a step forward, swing the tiptoe outward, bend the knee of the left leg with the heel out of the ground. At the same time, change the left palm into fist, draw it back and hold on the waist, with the fist – palm up: stretch the right palm forward, turn over the wrist outward for grabbing, and change into the mantis hook, with the tip of the hook down at the shoulder height. Eyes look forward
(Figure 4)

圖5

(2)上動不停。身體下蹲略向右轉；成半歇步；同時，右鉤手向後刁拉回帶，鉤尖向下置於右肩前；左拳食指、中指分開伸出變為剪子手，並向前方平插，指尖向前，手心向下；目視左手。（圖5）

(2) Keep the above action, the body squats and turns to the right slightly, change into the half rest stance. At the same time, pull the right hand in hook posture backward, with the tip of the hook down and putting before the right shoulder; separate forefinger and middle fingers to stretch and change into scissor hand, insert forward, with the finger tip forward and the palm down. Eyes look at the left hand.（Figure 5）

圖6

(3)上動不停。身體略向上提；同時，左剪子手在胸前向裏封抓變拳，拳心向下，拳面向右，高與肩平；目視前方。（圖6）

(3) Keep the above action, lift the body upward slightly. At the same time, the left scissor hand grab inward before the chest and change into fist, with the fist－palm down and the fist－plane rightward at the shoulder height. Eyes look forward.（Figure 6）

圖 7

　　(4)上動不停。左腳向前跨一步，右腳隨即跟步，
腳尖點地，身體下蹲成蹬山步；同時，左拳屈臂回收
於右胸前，拳心向下，拳面向右；右鉤手變為剪子手
向前平插，指尖向前，手心向下，高與肩平；目視右
手。（圖 7）

(4) Keep the above action, the left foot takes a step forward, then the right foot follows up with the tiptoe on the ground. The body squats to change into the mounta –ineering step. At the same time, bend the left arm, draw back the left fist before the right chest, with the fist –palm down, the striking surface of the fist –plane rightward; change the right hook hand into scissor hand and insert forward horizontally, with the finger tip forward and the palm down at the shoulder height. Eyes look at the right hand. (Figure 7)

七星螳螂拳白猿獻果

圖 8

3. 霸王甩鞭　Overlord swings whip

接上勢。左腳向前跨一步，右腳隨即跟步成玉環步；同時，右剪子手變拳，經左前臂內側收於腰間，隨即經胸前從右向左甩出，左拳與右拳一起向左甩出，兩拳心相對，高與肩平，右拳略低於左拳；目視前方。（圖8）

白
猿
獻
果
套
路
動
作
圖
解

Follow the above posture, the left foot takes a step forward, and the right one follows up to change into the jade −ring step. At the same time, change the right scissor hand into fist and draw it back on the waist through the inner side of the left forearm, then swing it from right to left through the front of the chest, the left fist, it swings leftward with the right hand, with the two fist−palm opposite at the shoulder height. Keep the right fist lower than the left one slightly. Eyes look forward. (Figure 8)

圖 9

4. 圈捶　Circle hammer

（1）接上勢。起身右轉 45°，重心移至兩腿間；同時，右拳變掌，向右、向上劃掌置於右前方，掌心向前，掌指向上，高與肩平；目視右掌。（圖 9）

（1）Follow the above posture, the body stands up and turns 45° to the right , move the barycenter between two legs. At the same time, change the right fist into palm to pull rightward and upward and put at the right ahead, with the palm forward and the fingers up at the shoulder height. Eyes look at the right palm.（Figure 9）

圖 10

(2)上動不停。重心移至右腳，左腳收回，腳尖點地，左腿屈膝成左虛步；同時，左拳從外向裏圈捶，置於胸前，拳心向下，拳面向右，高與肩平；右掌向裏迎擊左前臂，掌心貼於左前臂內側，掌指向上。（圖 10）

(2) Keep the above action, shift the barycenter to the right foot, draw back the left foot with the tiptoe on the ground, bend the knee of the left leg into the left empty stance. At the same time, the left fist makes circular pounding inward from outside, put before the chest, with the fist–palm down and the fist–plane rightward at the shoulder height; the right palm counter–punch the left forearm inward, with the palm close to the inner side of the left forearm and the fingers upward. (Figure 10)

圖 11

5. 格肘上步戳捶
Parry with elbow, step forward and thrust hammer

(1)接上勢。左腳向左前方上半步，身體起立，重心落於兩腿間；同時，右掌變拳收抱於腰間，拳心向上；左拳屈臂向外格肘，拳眼向左，拳心向裏，高與頜平。（圖11）

(2) Follow the above posture, the left foot takes half a step to the left ahead, the body stands up with the barycenter between two legs. At the same time, change the right palm into fist, draw it back and hold on the waist, with the fist–palm up; bend the left arm to parry outward, with the fist–hole outward and the fist–palm inward at the chin height. (Figure 11)

白猿獻果套路動作圖解

圖12

(2)上動不停。身體略左轉,重心前移至左腳,左
腿屈膝,右腳向前上步,腳尖翹起成七星步。右拳向
前平沖,拳心向下,高與肩平;左拳變掌迎擊右拳
面,附於右肘內側,掌指向上;目視前方。(圖12)

(2) Keep the above action, the body turns to the left slightly,
shift the barycenter to the left foot, bend the knee of the left leg,
the right foot steps forward with the tiptoe raising into the
seven-star stance. The right fist pushes forward horizontally,
with the fist-palm down at the shoulder height; change the left
fist into palm to counterpunch the fist-plane of the right fist,
attach to the inner side of the right elbow, with the fingers
upward. Eyes look forward. [Figure 12]

圖 13

6. 左封右崩捶
Left wrap and right snap hammer

(1)接上勢。右腳向前上半步踏實，身體提起，重心前移；同時，左手在胸前封抓變拳，拳心向下，高與肩平；右拳收抱於腰間，拳心向上；目視前方。（圖13）

(1) Follow the above posture, the right foot takes half a step forward and lands steadily, uplift the body and move the barycenter forward. At the same time, the left hand wraps to grab before the chest and change into fist, with the fist–palm down at the shoulder height; draw back the right fist and hold on the waist, with the fist–plane up. Eyes look forward.（Figure 13）

圖14

(2)上動不停。身體左轉 90°；同時，左拳屈臂回收於右胸前，拳心向下，拳面向右；右拳經左前臂內側向前反背崩拳，拳心向裏，拳面向上，高與頜平；目視右拳。（圖14）

(2) Keep the above action, the body turns 90° to the left. At the same time, bend the left arm and draw-back the left fist before the chest, with the fist-palm down and the fist-plane righttward; the right fist stretches forward for snap punch with its back through the inner side of the left forearm, with the fist-palm inward and the fist-plane up at the chin height. Eyes look at the right fist. (Figure 14)

圖 15

7. 撩陰捶
Upper-cut croth with hammer

(1)接上勢。右臂屈肘，右拳回收於胸前；同時，左拳經右前臂外側向上、向外挑掛於左肩前，兩拳心均向裏，拳面均向上；目視前方。（圖15）

(1) Follow the above posture, bend elbow of the right arm, draw back the right fist before the chest. At the same time, the left fist lift upward and outward to hang before the left shoulder through the outer side of the right forearm, with two fist–palms inward and the fist–planes up. Eyes look forward.〔Figure 15〕

白猿獻果套路動作圖解

圖 16

(2)上動不停。身微左轉，左腿向右後方插步；同時，左拳繼續向左上方格擋，拳心向上，拳面斜向上，高與頭頂平；右拳向右後方反撩，拳心向後，目視右後方。（圖 16）

(2) Keep the above action, the body turns to the left slightly, the left leg does the back cross stance rightward. At the same time, the left fist continue to parry to the left ahead, with the fist–palm up and the fist–plane up aslant at the head top height; the right fist raises back rightward, with the fist–palm backward. Eyes look back rightward. (Figure 16)

圖 17

8. 轉身圈捶秘肘

Turn about and circular hammer with secret elbow

（1）接上勢。起身向左轉 180°；同時，右臂向前掄，左臂向後掄，兩臂置於身體兩側，拳眼斜向下，拳心均向裏，高與胯平；目視左方。（圖 17）

（1）Follow the above posture, the body stands up and turns 180° to the left. At the same time, the right arm swings forward while the left one swings backward, put two arms at both sides of the body, with the fist–hole down aslant and the fist–palms inward at the hip level. Eyes look leftward.（Figure 17）

圖 18

(2)上動不停。身體繼續左轉 90°，重心前移；右
拳自外向裏圈捶，拳心向下，拳面向左，高與肩平；
左拳變掌迎擊右前臂，附於右前臂內側，掌心向右，
掌指向上；目視前方。（圖 18）

(2) Keep the above action, the body continues to turn 90° to
the left and move the barycenter. The right fist punches inward
from the outside, with the fist－palm down and the fist－plane
left ward at the shoulder height. Change the left fist into palm to
counterpunch the right forearm, with the palm outward and the
fingers upward. Eyes look forward.（Figure 18）

圖 19

(3)上動不停。右臂前伸，右手腕內翻抓握變拳，
拳心向下，拳面向左；目視右拳。（圖 19）

(3) Keep the above action, the right arm stretches forward,
turn over the right wrist inward, clench the right hand into fist,
with the fist–palm down and the fist–plane left ward. Eyes look
at the right fist.〔Figure 19〕

圖 20

（4）上動不停。左掌向前封抓變拳，拳心向下，拳面向右，高與肩平；右拳收抱於腰間，拳心向上；目視左拳。（圖 20）

(4) Keep the above action, the left palm wraps for-ward and change into fist, with the fist-palm down and the fist-plane ringht ward at the shoulder height; draw back the right fist and hold on the waist, with the fist-palm up. Eyes look at the left fist.〔Figure 20〕

七星螳螂拳白猿獻果

圖 21

(5)上動不停。左拳屈肘回收於右胸前；右拳經左拳上向前平沖，拳心向下，拳面向前，高與肩平；目視右拳。（圖 21）

(5) Keep the above action, bend the left elbow to draw back the left fist in front of the right chest; horiz –ontally punch the right fist forward, keep the fist –palm down and the fist –plane forward, at the shoulder level, Eyes look at the right fist. 〔Figure 21〕

圖 22

（6）上動不停。左拳變掌，經右臂外側向前推出，掌心向前，掌指向上，高與肩平；右拳變為螳螂鉤收於腰間，鉤尖向前；目視前方。（圖 22）

（6）Keep the above action, change the left fist into palm and push it forward through the outer side of the right arm, keep the palm forward and the fingers up, at the shoulder height; change the right one into mantis hook and draw it back on the waist; keep the hook-tip forward, Eyes look forward.（Figure 22）

圖 23

　　(7)上動不停。左腳向前上步，隨即右腳跟步，身
體下蹲；同時，左掌變鉤手向外鉤摟，鉤尖向左；右
鉤手自右向左、向前反背擊出，置於左膝上方，鉤尖
向下，呈秘肘勢；目視前方。（圖 23）

白
猿
獻
果
套
路
動
作
圖
解

(7)Keep the above action, the left foot steps forw-ard, then the right one follows up, the body squats down. At the same time, change the left palm into hook hand to grab outward, with the hook tip leftward; the right hook hand strikes leftward and forward from the right side with its back, put it above the left knee, with the hook tip down showing the posture of secret elbow. Eyes look forward. (Figure 23)

圖 24

第二段　Section Two

9. 轉身掄劈提剁
Turn over, swing, hack, lift and chop

⑴接上勢。身體起立，右轉身 180°，隨即右腿提膝，左腿獨立；同時，右鈎手變掌，隨身向上、向右、向後掄擺至右胯外側，掌心向外，掌指向下；左鈎手變掌，隨身向上掄擺於頭左上方，掌心向外，掌指向上；目視前方。（圖 24）

白
猿
献
果
套
路
動
作
圖
解

(1) Follow the above posture, the body stands up and turns 180° to the right, then lift the knee of the right leg with the left one standing alone. At the same time, change the right hook hand into palm, then swing to the outer side of the right hip upward, rightward and backward along with the body, with the palm outward and the fingers down; change the left hook hand into palm to swing to the overhead leftward, with the palm outward and the fingers up. Eyes look forward. (Figure 24)

圖 25

(2)上動不停。右腳向前落步，左腳隨即跟步成蹬
山步；同時，左掌向前按掌，屈肘收於胸前，掌心向
下；右掌向上、向前掄臂劈掌，掌刃向前，掌指向
上，高與肩平；目視右掌。（圖 25）

(2) Keep the above action, the right foot falls for-ward,
then the left foot follows up to change into the mountaineering
step. At the same time, the left palm presses forward, bend
elbow to draw before the chest, with the palm down; swing the
right arm and the right palm hacks upward and forward, with the
palm edge forward and the fingers upward at the shoulder height.
Eyes look at the right palm.（Figure 25）

圖 26

(3)上動不停。身體起立，右腿抬起；同時，右臂微屈，右掌變為螳螂鉤上提，鉤尖向下，略高於肩；目視前方。（圖 26）

(3)Keep the above action, the body stands up to lift the right foot. At the same time, bend the right arm slightly, change the right palm into mantis hook to lift up, with the hook tip down, higher than the shoulder slightly. Eyes look forward. ﹝ Figure 26 ﹞

圖 27

(4)上動不停。右腳向前落步，左腳隨即跟步成蹬山步；同時，右鉤手變掌向前劈掌，掌刃向前，掌指向上，高與肩平；目視右掌。（圖 27）

(4) Keep the above action, the right foot lands for–ward, then the left one follows up to change into the mountaineering step. At the same time, change the right hook hand into palm to hack forward, with the palm edge forward and the fingers up at the shoulder level. Eyes look at the right palm.（Figure 27）

圖 28

(5)上動不停。身體起立，右腿抬起；同時，右臂微屈，右掌變為螳螂鉤上提，鉤尖向下，略高於肩；目視前方。（圖 28）

(5)Keep the above action, the body stands up to lift the right leg. At the same time, bend the right arm slightly, change the right palm into mantis hook to lift up, with the hook tip down, higher than the shoulder slightly. Eyes look forward. ﹝Figure 28﹞

圖 29

(6)上動不停。右腳向前落步，左腳隨即跟步成蹬山步；同時，右鉤手變掌向前劈掌，掌刃向前，掌指向上，高與肩平；目視右掌。（圖 29）

(6) Keep the above action, the right foot lands for—ward, then the left one follows up to change into the mountaineering step. At the same time, change the right hook hand into palm to hack forward, with the palm edge forward and the fingers up at the shoulder height. Eyes look at the right palm.（Figure 29）

白猿獻果套路動作圖解

圖30

(7)上動不停。身體起立，右腿抬起；同時，右臂微屈，右掌變為螳螂鉤上提，鉤尖向下，略高於肩；目視前方。（圖30）

(7)Keep the above action, the body stands up to lift the right leg. At the same time, bend the right arm slightly, change the right palm into mantis hook to lift up, with the hook tip down, higher than the shoulder. Eyes look forward. (Figure 30)

圖 31

(8)上動不停。右腳向前落步，左腳隨即跟步成蹬
山步；同時，右鉤手變掌向前劈掌，掌刃向前，掌指
向上，高與肩平；目視右掌。（圖 31）

(8) Keep the above action, the right foot lands for–ward,
then the left one follows up to change into the mountaineering
step. At the same time, change the right hook hand into palm to
hack forward, with the palm edge forward and the fingers up at
the shoulder height. Eyes look at the right palm.（Figure 31）

圖 32

10. 三抹眉　Smear eyebrow three times

（1）接上勢。身體稍微上提，右掌收回腰間，掌心向下；左掌向前推按，掌心向下，掌指向右，略低於肩；目視左掌。（圖 32）

(1) Follow the above action, the body lifts up slightly, draw back the right palm on the waist, with the palm down; the left palm push forward and restrin, with the palm down and the fingers rightward, lower than the eyebrow slightly. eyes look at the left palm.（Figure 32）

圖 33

(2)上動不停。身體起立，略微左轉，左腳踏實；
同時，右掌從右向左平掃，掌心向下，掌指向前，高
與眉齊；左掌回收於左腰側，掌心向下；目視右掌。
（圖 33）

(2) Keep the above action, the body stands up and turns to
the left slightly, the left foot stamps steadily. At the same time,
the right palm sweeps horizontally from right to left, with the
palm down and the fingers forward at the eyebrow height; draw
back the left palm on the side of the left waist, with the palm
down. Eyes look at the right palm. (Figure 33)

圖 34

(3)上動不停。身體右轉 90°，左腳尖點地；同時，左掌從左向右平掃，掌心向下，掌指向前，高與眉齊；右掌回收於右腰側，掌心向下；目視左掌。（圖 34）

(3) Keep the above action, the body turns 90° to the right with the left tiptoes on the ground. At the same time, the left palm sweeps horizontally from left to right, with the palm down and the fingers forward at the eyebrow height; draw back the right palm on the side of the right waist, with the palm down. Eyes look at the left palm. (Figure 34)

圖 35

（4）上動不停。身體左轉 90°，向下蹲身成馬步；
同時，右掌從右向左平掃，屈臂抱於胸前；左臂屈肘
抱於胸前，左臂在裏，右臂在外，兩掌心均向下，掌
指均向外；目視右方。（圖 35）

白
猿
獻
果
套
路
動
作
圖
解

(4)Keep the above action, the body turns 90° to the left, the body squats into the horse stance. At the same time, the right palm sweeps horizontally from right to left, bend the arm to hold before the chest; bend elbow of the left arm to hold before the chest, with the left arm inside, the right one outside, two palms down and the fingers outward. Eyes look rightward. (Figure 35)

圖 36

11. 蓋陽掌玉環步
Cover with Yang-palm in jade-ring step

（1）接上勢。身體起立，右轉 180°，左腳跟提起，重心前移成交叉步；同時，右掌收於腰間，掌心向上；左掌從右臂外側向前反蓋掌，掌心向上，掌指向前，高與頭頂平；目視左掌。（圖 36）

白
猿
獻
果
套
路
動
作
圖
解

(1) Follow the above posture, the body stands up and forward turns 180° to the right, lift the left heel, shift the barycenter into the cross stance. At the same time, draw back the right palm on the waist, with the palm up; the left palm stretches forward for back covering from the outer side of the right arm, with the palm up and the fingers forward at the head top height. Eyes look at the left palm. (Figure 36)

七星螳螂拳白猿獻果

圖 37

　(2)上動不停。左腳向前上一步，右腳隨即跟步，身體下蹲成玉環步；同時，左掌變拳，左臂屈肘向左拉帶，掌心向下，拳眼向右，高與肩平；右掌向左下方推掌，置於左膝外側，掌心向左，掌指向前；目視左前方。（圖 37）

　(2) Keep the above action, the left foot takes a step forward, then the right foot follows up to change into the jade–ring step. At the same time, change the left palm into fist, bend elbow of the left arm and pull leftward, with the fist–palm down and the palm hole ringnt ward at the shoulder height; push the right palm teft downward horizontally and put at the outer side of the left knee. with the palm leftward and the fingers forward. Eyes look forward.（Figure 37）

圖 38

12. 左封右崩捶
Left wrap and right snap hammer

(1)接上勢。右腳向前上一步，左腳隨即跟步成蹬山步；左手向裏封抓變拳，拳心向下，拳面向右，高與肩平；右掌變拳收抱於腰間；目視向方。（圖 38 ）

(1) Follow the above posture, the right foot takes a step forward, the left one follows up to change into the mountaineering step. The left hand warps inward and change into fist, with the fist–palm down and the fist–plane rightward at the shoulder height; change the right palm into fist, draw it back and hold on the waist. Eyes look forward. (Figure 38)

圖 39

(2)上動不停。左拳收於胸前，拳面向下；右拳向前反背崩出，拳心向裏，拳面向上，高與頜平；目視右拳。（圖 39）

(2) Keep the above action, draw back the left fist before the chest. with fist–plane down; the right fist snaps forward in its back, with the fist–palm inward and the fist–plane up at the chin height. Eyes look at the right fist.（Figure 39）

圖 40

13. 千眼鴛鴦腳
Thousand-eye mandarin duck foot

（1）接上勢。身體提起，左轉 90°；同時，左拳變掌，經右臂外側向上、向外推出，掌心向前，高與肩平；目視左掌。（圖 40）

(1) Follow the above posture, the body stands up and turns 90° to the left. At the same time, change the left fist into palm and push upward and outward through the outer side of the right arm, with the palm forward at the shoulder height. Eyes look at the left palm.〔Figure 40〕

圖 41

（2）上動不停。右拳變掌，兩掌同時向右、向上、向左劃圓，變為螳螂鉤。左鉤手置於左胯旁，鉤尖向下；右鉤手置於胸前，鉤尖向右；目視右鉤手。（圖41）

（2）Keep the above action, change the right fist into palm, two palms pull circles rightward, forward and left –ward and change into the mantis hook. Put the left hook hand near the left hip, with the hook tip downward; put the right hook hand before the chest, with the hook tip rightward. Eyes look at the right look hand.（Figure 41）

白猿獻果套路動作圖解

圖 42

(3)上動不停。重心後移至左腿，右腿抬起，以腳尖向右上方點擊；同時，右鉤手向右反背勾擊，兩鉤尖均向右；目視右腳。（圖 42）

(3) Keep the above action, move the barycenter to the left leg, lift the right leg and the tiptoes strike rightward up. At the same time, the right hook hands strike rightward in their back, with the hook tip rightward. Eyes look at the right foot. 〔 Figure 42 〕

圖 43

14. 閉手　Close-up　hand

(1)接上勢。右腿屈膝收回，成左獨立勢；同時，右鉤手收於胸前，鉤尖向下；目視右前方。（圖 43）

(1) Follow the above posture, bend the knee of the right leg and draw back to change into the posture of standing on the left leg. At the same time, draw back the right hook hand before the chest, with the hook tip down. Eyes look right forward.（Figure 43）

圖 44

(2)上動不停。左腿彎曲，身體向左側下坐。（圖 44）

(2) Keep the above action, bend the left leg, the body squats down leftward.〔Figure 44〕

七星螳螂拳白猿獻果

圖 45

(3)上動不停。右腳向下落步，隨即身體右轉90°，左腳向後撤步，左腿屈膝成虛實步；同時，兩鉤手變掌，向左回帶於左腰側，隨即右掌反掌向右格掌，掌心斜向上，高與頜平；左掌附於右肘內側，掌心向下，掌指向右；目視右掌。（圖45）

白
猿
獻
果
套
路
動
作
圖
解

(3) Keep the above action, the right foot falls down, then the body turns 90° to the right, the left foot steps backward and bend the knee of the left leg into the empty – solid step. At the same time, change two hook hands into palm and pull back at the side of the left waist, then turn over the right palm rightward to parry the palm, with the palm up aslant at the chin height; attach the left palm to the inner side of the right elbow, with the palm down and the fingers rightward. Eyes look at the right palm. (Figure 45)

圖 46

15. 左右紉針
Thread needle to the left and right

(1)接上勢。身微右轉，右腳向前上半步，重心前移成右高弓步；同時，右掌回收，翻掌下按於胸前，掌心向下，掌指向左；左掌經右前臂內側向前平穿掌，掌心向右，掌指向前，高與肩平；目視左掌。（圖 46）

白
猿
獻
果
套
路
動
作
圖
解

(1) Follow the above posture, the body turns to the right slightly, the right foot takes a half –step forward, transfer the barycenter forward to change into the right high bow stance. At the same time, draw back the right palm, turn over the palm and press before the chest, with the palm rightward and fingers leftward at the shou –lder height. Eyes look at the left palm. (Figure 46)

圖 47

　　(2)上動不停。左掌回收，翻掌下按於胸前，掌心向下，掌指向右；右掌經左前臂內側向前平穿掌，掌心向左，掌指向前，高與肩平；目視右掌。（圖 47）

　　(2) Keep the above action, draw back the left palm, turn over and press before the chest, with the palm down and the fingers rightward; thread out the right palm forward horizontally through the inner side of the left forearm; with the palm leftward and the fingers forward at the shoulder height. Eyes look at the right palm.（Figure 47）

圖48

16. 玉環步　Jade-ring step

(1)接上勢。身體略右轉，左腳跟抬起，重心前移至右腳；同時，左掌經右臂外側向前穿掌，掌心向右，掌指向前，略高於肩；右掌回抱於腰間，掌心向上；目視左掌。（圖48）

(1) Follow the above posture, the body turns to the right slightly, lift the left heel and transfer the barycenter forward to the right foot. At the same time, thread out the left palm forward through the outer side of the right arm, with the palm rightward and the fingers forward, higher than the shoulder slightly; draw back the right palm and hold on the waist, with the palm up. Eyes look at the left palm. (Figure 48)

圖 49

　　(2)上動不停。左腳向左前方上步，右腳隨即跟步，蹲身成玉環步；同時，左掌翻腕變拳，屈臂向左回帶，拳心向下，拳眼向裏，高與肩平；右掌自右向左下方平推，置於左膝外側，掌心向左，掌指向前；目視左前方。（圖 49）

白
猿
獻
果
套
路
動
作
圖
解

(2) Keep the above action, the left foot steps left forward, the right one follows up and squat the body into the jade-ring step. At the same time, turn over the wrist of the left palm and change into fist, bend the arm and pull back leftward, with the fist-palm down and the fist-hole inward at the shoulder height; push the right palm downward horizontally from right to left, put at the outer side of the left knee, with the palm leftward and the fingers forward. Eyes look left forward. (Figure 49)

圖 50

第三段　Section Three

17. 轉身霸王甩鞭
Overlord turns and swings whip

(1)接上勢。身體右轉 180°，右腳略上半步，重心移至兩腿間；同時，左拳置於身後，拳心向下，右掌隨身經胸前擺掌上托，掌心向上，兩手高與肩平，兩臂呈水平；目視右前方。（圖 50）

白
猿
獻
果
套
路
動
作
圖
解

(1) Follow the above posture, the body turns 180° to the right, the right foot takes a half –step forward slightly and transfer the barycenter between two legs. At the same time, put the left fist at the back of the body, with the fist –palm down; swing the right palm forward to lift through the front of the chest, with the palm up. Keep two hands high with the shoulder and two arms horizo–ntal. Eyes look forward. (Figure 50)

圖 51

(2)上動不停。身體右擰 90°，左腳跟抬起，重心
前移至右腿；同時，右手抓握變拳收抱於腰間，拳心
向上；左拳從後向前、向上抄拳，拳心斜向上，拳眼
向左，高與頭頂平；目視左拳。（圖 51）

(2) Keep the above action, the body twists to the right by
90°, lift the left heel, transfer the barycenter to the right leg. At
the same time, clench the right hand into fist, draw it back and
hold on the waist, with the fist–palm up; lift the left fist forward
and upward from back, with the fist –palm up aslant and the
fist–hole left ward at the head top level. Eyes look at the left fist.
(Figure 51)

白猿獻果套路動作圖解

圖 52

(3)上動不停。左腳向前上步，右腳隨即跟步，身
體下蹲成玉環步；同時，左臂內旋，右臂前伸，隨即
兩臂向左橫掃，兩拳心相對；目視前方。（圖 52）

(3) Keep the above action, the left foot steps for−ward, then
the right one follows up, the body squats down into the jade−
ring step. At the same time, whirl the left arm inward, the right
arm stretches forward, then the two arms sweep leftward
horizontally, with the fist −palms opposite. Eyes look left
forward.（Figure 52）

圖 53

18. 左封右崩捶
Left wrap and right snap hammer

（1）接上勢。右腳向前上步，隨即左腳跟步成蹬山步；同時，右拳收抱於腰間，拳心向上；左手向裏封抓變拳，拳心向下，拳眼向裏，高與肩平；目視左拳。（圖 53）

(1) Follow the above posture, the right foot steps for–ward, then the left one follows up to change into the mountaineering step. At the same time, draw back the right fist and hold on the waist, with the fist–palm up; the left hand wraps inward into fist, with the fist –palm down and the fist –hole inward at the shoulder level. Eyes look at the left fist.（Figure 53）

圖 54

（2）上動不停。左拳回收於右胸前，拳心向下，拳面向右；右拳經左前臂內側向前崩拳，拳心向裏，拳面向上，高與頜平；目視右拳。（圖 54）

（2）Keep the above action, draw back the left fist before the right chest, with the fist–palm down and the fist–plane up at the chin heigh. Eyes look at the right fist.〔Figure 54〕

七星螳螂拳白猿獻果

圖 55

19. 採三手玉環步
Grab hand three times in jade-ring step

（1）接上勢。身體重心略微上提；同時，右手向外翻腕採抓變拳，拳心斜向下，拳面向前，高與肩平。（圖 55）

(1) Follow the above posture, uplift the barycenter of the body upward slightly, at the same time, turn over the wrist of the right hand outward to grab and change into fist, with the fist – palm down aslant and the fist – plane of the fist forward at the shoulder height.（Figure 55）

圖 56

(2)上動不停。身體略微右轉成右弓步；同時，右拳收抱於腰間，拳心向上；左拳變掌，從胸前向前封抓變拳，拳心向下，拳面向右，高與肩平；目視左拳。（圖 56）

(2) Keep the above action, the body turns to the right slightly into the right bow stance. At the same time, draw back the right fist and hold on the waist, with the fist –palm up; change the left fist into palm and wrap forward from the front of the chest to change into fist, with the fist –palm down and the fist–plane of the fist rightward at the shoulder height. Eyes look at the left fist. (Figure 56)

七星螳螂拳白猿獻果

圖 57

(3)上動不停。身體起立，略向左轉；同時，右拳經左前臂內側向前上方沖出，拳心斜向上，高與眼齊；左拳回收於右胸前，拳心向下；目視右拳。（圖57）

(3) Keep the above action, the body stands up and turns to the left slightly. At the same time, the right fist strikes forward through the inner side of the left forearm, with the fist–palm up aslant at the eye height; draw back the left fist before the chest, with the fist–palm down. Eyes look at the right fist.〔Figure 57〕

圖 58

(4)上動不停。身體向右擰轉 90°；右拳收回抱於腰間，拳心向上；左拳變掌，經右臂外側向前穿掌，掌心斜向上，掌指向左前方；目視左掌。（圖 58）

(4) Keep the above action, the body twists 90° to the right, draw back the right fist and hold on the waist, with the fist–palm up; change the left fist into palm and thread forward through the outer side of the right arm, with the palm up aslant and the fingers left forward. Eyes look at the left palm. 〔 Figure 58 〕

七星螳螂拳白猿獻果

圖 59

　(5)上動不停。左腳向前跨一步，隨即右腳跟步，身體向左擰轉 90°，蹲身成玉環步；同時，左掌翻腕變拳向左側拉帶，拳心向下，高與肩平；右拳變掌，經胸前向左下方推掌，置於左膝外側，掌心向左，掌指向前；目視左前方。（圖 59）

白
猿
獻
果
套
路
動
作
圖
解

(5) Keep the above action, the left foot strides a step forward, then the right one follows up, the body twists 90° to the left and squat down into the jade-ring step. At the same time, turn over the twist of the left palm, change into fist and pull leftward, with the fist-palm down at the shoulder height; change the right fist into palm to push left downard horizontally through the front of the chest, put at the outer side of the left knee, with the palm leftward and the fingers forward. Eyes look left forward. (Figure 59)

圖 60

第四段　Section Four

20. 轉身連環戳捶

Turn around and thrust interlink hammer

⑴接上勢。身體右轉 180°，左腿獨立，右腿提膝；同時，左拳收抱於腰間，拳心向上；右手翻腕變掌，掌心向下，置於左胸前方；目視右前方。（圖60）

白
猿
獻
果
套
路
動
作
圖
解

(1) Follow the above posture, The body turns 180° to the right, the left leg stands alone, lift the knee of the right leg. At the same time, draw back the left fist and hold on the waist, with the fist–palm up; turn over the wrist of the left hand to change into the palm down, put in front of the left chest. Eyes look right forward. (Figure 60)

圖 61

(2)上動不停。重心前移，右腳向前落步；同時，右掌經胸前向右摟抓，高與肩平；目視右掌。（圖61）

(2) Keep the above action, transfer the barycenter fo‒rward and right foot lands forward. At the same time, the right palm grab rightward through the front of the chest, with the palm down at the shoulder height. Eyes look at the right palm.（Figure 61）

圖 62

　（３）上動不停。身體右轉 90°，左腳跟步，向下蹲身成蹬山步；同時，右拳收抱於腰間，拳心向上；左拳向前立拳沖出，拳眼向上，高與肩平；目視左拳。（圖 62）

　（3) Keep the above action, the body turns 90° to the right, the left foot follows up and the body squats into the mountaineering stance. At the same time, draw back the right fist and hold on the waist, with the fist–palm up; the left fist strikes forward with the standing fist, with the fist–hole upward at the shoulder level. Eyes look at the left fist.（Figure 62）

七星螳螂拳白猿獻果

圖 63

(4)上動不停。右腳向前上步，左腳隨即跟步，身體左轉 90°成馬步；同時，左拳變掌收於右胸前，掌心向右，掌指向上；右拳向右平沖，拳心向下，高與肩平；目視右拳。（圖 63）

(4) Keep the above action, the right foot steps for-ward, then the left one follows up, the body turns 90° to the left to change into the horse stance. At the same time, change the left fist into palm and draw back before the right chest, with the palm rightward and the fingers up; the right fist strikes forward horizontally, with the fist-palm down at the shoulder height. Eyes look at the right fist.（Figure 63）

白猿獻果套路動作圖解

圖 64

(5)上動不停。身體右轉 90°，右腳向前上步，左
腳隨即跟步，向下蹲身成蹬山步；同時，右拳收抱於
腰間，拳心向上；左拳向前立拳沖出，拳眼向上，高
與肩平；目視前方。（圖 64）

(5) Keep the above action, the body turns 90° to the right,
the right foot steps forward, then the left one follows up, the
body squats into the mountaineering step. At the same time,
draw back the right fist and hold on the waist, with the fist–palm
up; the left fist strikes forward with the standing fist, with the
fist–hole up at the shoulders height. Eyes look forward.（Figure
64）

圖 65

　　(6)上動不停。右腳向前上步，左腳隨即跟步，身
體左轉 90°成馬步；同時，左拳變掌收於右胸前，掌心
向右，掌指向上；右拳向右平沖，拳心向下，高與肩
平；目視右拳。（圖 65）

白
猿
獻
果
套
路
動
作
圖
解

(6) Keep the above action, the right foot steps forw –ard, then left foot follows up, the body turns 90° to the left into the horse stance. At the same time, change the left fist into palm and draw back before the right chest, with the palm rightward and the fingers up; the right fist strikes rightward horizontally, with the fist–palm down at the shoulder height. Eyes look at the right fist. (Figure 65)

圖 66

21. 左封右崩捶
Left wrap and right snap hammer

(1)接上勢。身體右轉 90°，右腳向前上步，左腳隨即跟步，向下蹲身成蹬山步；同時，右拳收抱於腰間，拳心向上；左手向裏封抓變拳，拳心向下，拳眼向裏，高與肩平；目視前方。（圖 66）

白
猿
獻
果
套
路
動
作
圖
解

(1) Follow the above posture, the body turns 90° to the right, the right foot steps forward, then the left one follows up, the body squats into the mountaineering step. At the same time, draw back the right fist and hold on the waist, with the fist–palm up; the left hand warps inward to clench into fist, with the fist–palm down and the fist–hole inward at the shoulder height. Eyes look forward. (Figure 66)

七
星
螳
螂
拳
白
猿
獻
果

圖 67

(2)上動不停。左拳回收於右胸前，拳心向下，拳面向右；右拳經左前臂內側向前崩拳，拳心向裏，拳面向上，高與頜平；目視右拳。（圖 67）

(2) Keep the above action, draw back the left fist before the right chest, with the fist –palm down and the fist –plane rightward; the right fist snaps forward through the inner side of the left forearm, with the fist–palm inward and the fist–plane up at the chin height. Eyes look at the right fist.（Figure 67）

白猿獻果套路動作圖解

圖 68

22. 探三手玉環步
Grab hand three times in jade-ring step

(1) 接上勢。身體重心略微上提；同時，右手向外翻腕採抓變拳，拳心斜向下，拳面向前，高與肩平。（圖 68）

(1) Follow the above posture, lift the barycenter of the body slightly, at the same time, turn over the wrist of the right hand to grab into fist, with the fist-palm down aslant and the fist-plane forward at the shoulder height.（Figure 68）

圖 69

（2）上動不停。身體略微右轉；同時，右拳收抱於腰間，拳心向上；左拳變掌，從胸前向前封抓變拳，拳心向下，拳面向右，高與肩平；目視左拳。（圖69）

（2）Keep the above action, the body turns to the right slightly. At the same time, draw back the right fist and hold on the waist, with the fist–palm up; change the left fist into palm to wrap for grab forward from the front of the chest and change into fist, with the fist–palm down and the fist–plane rightward at the shoulder level. Eyes look at the left fist.〔Figure 69〕

白猿獻果套路動作圖解

圖 70

(3)上動不停。身體起立，略向左轉；同時，右拳
經左前臂內側向前上方沖出，拳心斜向上，高與眼
齊；左拳回收於右胸前，拳心向下；目視右拳。（圖
70）

(3) Keep the above action, the body stands up and turns to
the left slightly. At the same time, the right fist thrusts forward
through the inner side of the right for-earm, with the fist-palm
up at the eye height; draw back the left fist before the right chest,
with the fist-palm down. Eyes look at the right fist. (Figure
70)

圖 71

（4）上動不停。身體向右擰轉 90°，右拳收回抱於腰間，拳心向上；左拳變掌，經右臂外側向前穿掌，掌心向右，掌指向左前方；目視左掌。（圖 71）

（4）Keep the above action, the body twists 90° to the right, draw back the right fist and hold on the waist, with the fist-palm up; change the left fist into palm to thread forward through the outer side of the right arm, with the palm right aslant and the fingers left forward. Eyes look at the left palm.（Figure 71）

圖 72

（5）上動不停。左腳向前上步，隨即右腳跟步，身
體向左擰轉 90°，蹲身成玉環步；同時，左掌翻腕變
拳，向左側拉帶，拳心向下，高與肩平；右拳變掌，
經胸前向左下方推掌，置於左膝外側，掌心向左，掌
指向前；目視左前方。（圖 72）

（5）Keep the above action, the left foot steps for−ward, then
the right one follows up, the body twists 90° to the left and
squats into the jade−ring step. At the same time, turn over the
twist of the left palm to change into fist and pull leftward, with
the fist−palm down at the shoulder height; change the right fist
into palm to push left downward horizontally through the front
of the chest and put at the outer side of the left knee, with the
palm leftward and the fingers forward. Eyes look left forward.
（Figure 72）

圖 73

23. 橫掃千軍雙封手
Sweep and wrap with hands

(1)接上勢。身體重心提起，右轉 90°，右腳向後倒插步；同時，左拳擺向身後，拳眼斜向下；右掌翻腕成掌心向下，置於胸前；目視左下方。（圖 73）

(1) Follow the above posture, lift the barycenter of the body and turn it 90° to the right, the right foot does back cross step. At the same time, the left fist swings back of the body, with the fist–hole down aslant; turn over the wrist of the right palm into the palm down and put before the chest. Eyes look left downward. (Figure 73)

白猿獻果套路動作圖解

圖 74

(2)上動不停，身體右轉 180°，重心落於兩腿間；
同時，左拳變掌向前平掃；右掌經胸前向右平掃，右
掌指向右，左掌指向前，兩掌心均向下，高與肩平。
（圖 74）

(2) Keep the above action, the body turns180° to the right,
with the barycenter between two legs. At the same time, change
the left fist into palm to sweep for–ward horizontally; the right
palm sweeps rightward thr–ough the front of the chest, with the
fingers of the right palm rightward while that of the left one
forward and two palms down at the shoulder height. (Figure
74)

圖 75

（3）上動不停。身體左轉 90°，重心前移成左弓
步；右掌翻腕成掌心向上，經腰間向前穿掌，掌指向
前，高與肩平；左掌收於右肘下，掌心向下，掌指向
右；目視前方。（圖 75）

（3）Keep the above action, the body turns to the 90° to the
left, transfer the barycenter forward into the left bow stance.
Turn over the wrist of the right palm into the palm up and thread
out the palm forward through the waist, with the fingers forward
at the shoulder height; draw the left palm under the right elbow,
with the palm down and the fingers rightward. Eyes look
forward. (Figure 75)

白猿獻果套路動作圖解

圖 76

(4)上動不停。身體提起，重心後移至兩腿間；同時，右掌翻掌，兩掌交叉於腹前，右掌在外，左掌在裏，兩掌心均向下；目視兩掌。（圖 76）

(4) Keep the above action, uplift the body and tran–sfer the barycenter between two legs. At the same time, turn over the right palm, cross palms before abdomen, with the right palm outside, the left one inside and two palms down. Eyes look at the palms.〔Figure 76〕

圖 77

（5）上動不停。身體略向後傾斜；同時，兩臂屈肘，兩掌在胸前翻轉絞手，右掌心向上，掌指向右；左掌心向右，兩掌高與頜平；目視兩掌。（圖 77）

（5）Keep the above action, the body slants bac –kward slightly. At the same time, bend elbows of two arms, turn over two palms to twist the hands before the chest, with the right palm up, the fingers rightward and the left palm rightward. Keep the palms high with the jaw. Eyes lookat the palms.（Figure 77）

白猿獻果套路動作圖解

圖 78

(6)上動不停。重心略前移；同時，右掌前探，掌
心向前，虎口向上，高與肩平；左掌護於右肩前，掌
指向上，掌心向外；目視右掌。（圖 78）

(6) Keep the above action, transfer the barycenter forward
slightly. At the same time, the right palm stre –tches forward,
with the palm forward and tiger´s mouth up at the shoulder
height; the left palm guards before the right shoulder, with the
fingers up and the palm out –ward. Eyes look at the right palm.
（Figure 78）

圖79

(7)上動不停。右臂屈肘，右掌變為螳螂鉤，吊腕勾拉於胸前，鉤尖向右；同時，左掌向前探，掌心向外，掌指向前，高與肩平；目視左掌。（圖79）

(7) Keep the above action, bend the elbow of the right arm, change the right palm into mantis hook, hand the wrist to pull before the chest, with the hook tip righ-tward. At the same time, the left palm stretches forward, with the palm outward and the fingers forward at the shoulder height. Eyes look at the left palm. (Figure 79)

白
猿
獻
果
套
路
動
作
圖
解

圖 80

(8)上動不停。身體下蹲；同時，左臂屈肘，左鈎
手吊腕回拉於左膝上方，略低於肩；目視左前方。
（圖 80）

(8) Keep the above action, the body squats down. At the
same time, bend the elbow of the left arm, hang the wrist of the
left hook hand to pull back above the left knee, lower than the
shoulder slightly. Eyes look left forward.（Figure 80）

圖 81

24. 收勢　Closing form

(1)接上勢。身體右轉 90°成馬步；同時，兩鉤手變掌，經胸前上托，隨即向兩側分掌，兩臂成水平，兩掌心向外，掌指向上；目視右掌。（圖 81 ）

(1)Follow the above posture, the body turns 90° to the right into the horse stance. At the same time, change two hook hands into palms to lift up through the front of the chest, then detach the palms to both sides, keep the arms horizontal, with the palms outward and the fingers up. Eyes look at the right palm. (Figure 81)

白猿献果套路動作圖解

圖 82

(2)上動不停。身體重心提起,左腳向右腳併步; 同時,兩掌變拳抱於腰間;目視前方。（圖 82）

(2) Keep the above action, lift the barycenter of the body, bring the left foot and right one together. At the same time, change the palms into fists and hold on the waist. Eyes look forward.〔 Figure 82 〕

圖 83

(3)上動不停。兩拳變掌，自然下垂於身體兩側；目視前方。（圖 83）

要點：挺胸收腹，平心靜氣，體態自然，精神內斂。

(3) Keep the above action, change the fists into pal-ms and drop on both side of the body naturally. Eyes look forward. (Figure 83)

Key points: lift the chest, draw in the abdomen, calmly, posture is natural and vital energy collects inward.

全套動作示意圖
Demonstration of All the Actions

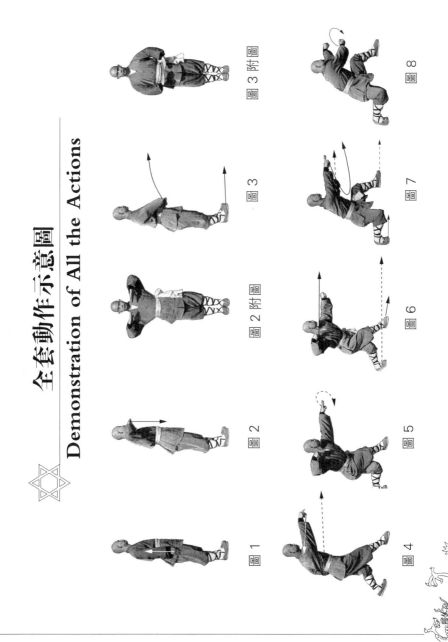

圖3附圖

圖3

圖2附圖

圖2

圖1

圖8

圖7

圖6

圖5

圖4

全套動作示意圖

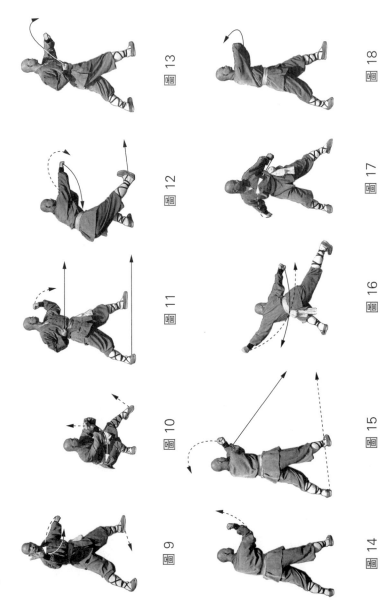

图13　图18　图12　图17　图11　图16　图10　图15　图9　图14

圖 23

圖 28

圖 22

圖 27

圖 21

圖 26

圖 20

圖 25

圖 19

圖 24

全套動作示意圖

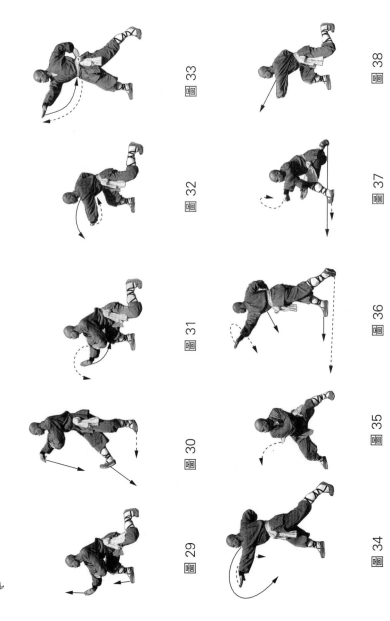

圖 33

圖 32

圖 31

圖 30

圖 29

圖 38

圖 37

圖 36

圖 35

圖 34

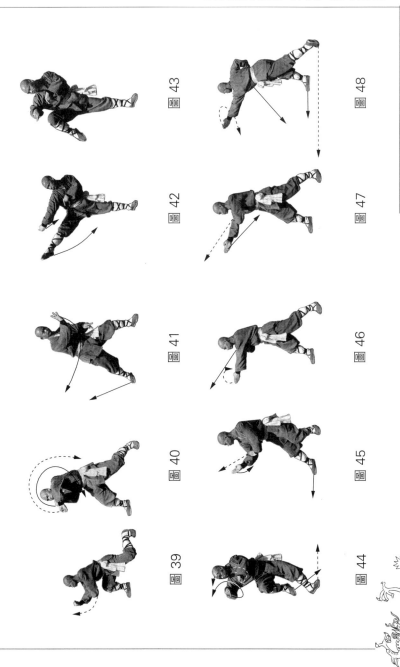

圖 43　圖 42　圖 41　圖 40　圖 39

圖 48　圖 47　圖 46　圖 45　圖 44

全套動作示意圖

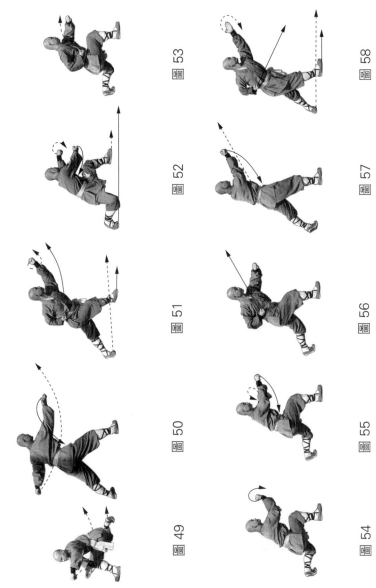

図 53

図 52

図 51

図 50

図 49

図 58

図 57

図 56

図 55

図 54

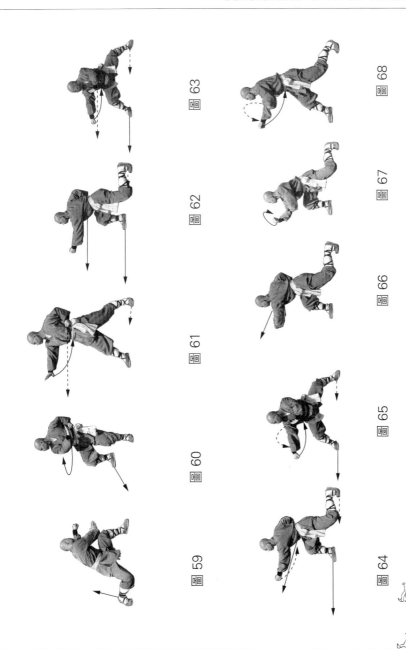

全套動作示意圖

圖 63

圖 62

圖 61

圖 60

圖 59

圖 68

圖 67

圖 66

圖 65

圖 64

七星螳螂拳白猿獻果

圖73

圖72

圖71

圖70

圖69

圖78

圖77

圖76

圖75

圖74

圖 83

圖 82

圖 81

圖 80

圖 79

全套動作示意圖

導引養生功 系列叢書

張廣德養生著作

每冊定價 350 元

全系列為彩色圖解附教學光碟

彩色圖解太極武術

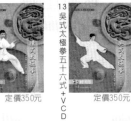

太極跤

1 太極防身術

定價300元

2 擒拿術

定價280元

3 中國式摔角

定價350元

簡化太極拳

1 陳式太極拳十三式

定價200元

2 楊式太極拳十三式

定價200元

3 吳式太極拳十三式

定價200元

4 武式太極拳十三式

定價200元

5 孫式太極拳十三式

定價200元

6 趙堡太極拳十三式

定價200元

原地太極拳

1 原地綜合太極二十四式

定價220元

2 原地活步太極四十二式

定價200元

3 原地簡化太極拳二十四式

定價200元

4 原地太極拳十二式

定價200元

5 原地青少年太極拳二十二式

定價220元

6 原地兒童太極拳十播十六式

定價180元

健康加油站

1　糖尿病預防與治療

定價200元

2　胃部機能與強健

定價180元

3　不孕症治療

定價200元

4　簡易醫學急救法

定價200元

5　肥胖健康診療

定價200元

6　肝功能健康診療

定價200元

7　高血壓健康診療

定價200元

8　高血糖值健康診療

定價200元

9　尿酸值健康診療

定價200元

10　膽固醇中性脂肪健康診療

定價200元

11　痛風劇痛消除法

定價180元

12　三溫暖健康法

定價180元

13　手‧腳病理按摩

定價180元

14　B型肝炎預防與治療

定價180元

15　吃得更漂亮．健康

定價180元

16　茶使您更健康

定價180元

17　圖解常見疾病運動療法

定價180元

18　科學健身改變亞健康

定價180元

運動精進叢書

1 怎樣跑得快
定價200元

2 怎樣投得遠
定價180元

3 怎樣跳得遠
定價180元

4 怎樣跳的高
定價180元

5 高爾夫揮桿原理
定價220元

6 網球技巧圖解
定價220元

7 東式太極拳十三式
排球技巧圖解
定價230元

8 沙灘排球技巧圖解
定價230元

9 撞球技巧圖解
定價230元

10 籃球技巧圖解
定價220元

11 足球技巧圖解
定價230元

快樂健美站

1 柔力健身球

定價200元

2 自行車健康享瘦
定價200元

3 跑步鍛鍊走路減肥
定價200元

4 創造健康的肌力訓練
定價200元

5 舒適超級伸展體操
定價200元

6 水中有氧運動
定價200元

7 雕塑完美身材

定價200元

8 創造超級兒童
定價200元

9 陳式太極拳十三式
定價200元

10 防止老化的身體改造訓練
定價200元

11 三個月塑身計畫

定價200元

12 懶人族瑜伽

定價200元

13 忙裡偷閒練瑜伽基礎篇

定價200元

14 忙裡偷閒練瑜伽祛病養生篇
定價200元

15 健身跑激發身體的潛能

定價200元

16 中華鐵球健身操
定價200元

17 彼拉提斯健身寶典

定價200元

19 瑜伽美姿美容

定價180元

國家圖書館出版品預行編目資料

七星螳螂拳白猿獻果╱耿　軍　著
　　　──初版，──臺北市，大展，2007〔民96〕
　　　面；21 公分，──（少林傳統功夫漢英對照系列；3）
　　　ISBN　978-957-468-526-4（平裝）

1.拳術──中國
528.97　　　　　　　　　　　　　　　　　96001551

七星螳螂拳白猿獻果　ISBN-13：978-957-468-526-4

著　　　者╱耿　軍
責任編輯╱孔 令 良
發 行 人╱蔡 森 明
出 版 者╱大展出版社有限公司
社　　　址╱台北市北投區（石牌）致遠一路 2 段 12 巷 1 號
電　　　話╱（02）28236031・28236033・28233123
傳　　　眞╱（02）28272069
郵政劃撥╱01669551
網　　　址╱www.dah-jaan.com.tw
E - mail ╱ service@dah-jaan.com.tw
登 記 證╱局版臺業字第 2171 號
承 印 者╱高星印刷品行
裝　　　訂╱建鑫印刷裝訂有限公司
排 版 者╱弘益電腦排版有限公司
授 權 者╱北京人民體育出版社
初版 1 刷╱2007 年（民 96 年）4 月

定　價╱180 元